Gertrude Lawrence
Oh, Kay! (1926)

The King and I
(1951)

PLATE 2

Vivienne Segal
Pal Joey (1940)

The Three Musketeers (1928)

PLATE 1

Beatrice "Bea" Lillie
Inside U.S.A.
(1948)

High Spirits
(1964)

Plate 3

Eve Arden
Ziegfeld Follies of 1934
(1934)

Let's Face It!
(1941)

PLATE 4

Gypsy Rose Lee
Ziegfeld Follies of 1936
(1936)

Star and Garter
(1942)

Do not cut out space between arm and body.

Celeste Holm
Bloomer Girl
(1944)

Oklahoma!
(1943)

PLATE 6

Nanette Fabray
Mr. President
(1962)

High Button Shoes
(1947)

PLATE 7

Nancy Walker
Copper and Brass
(1957)

Barefoot Boy With Cheek
(1947)

Do not cut out spaces between arms and body.

Barbara Cook
The Music Man
(1957)

Candide
(1956)

PLATE 9

Do not cut out space between arm and body.

Shirley Booth
A Tree Grows in Brooklyn
(1951)

By the Beautiful Sea
(1954)

PLATE 10

Elaine Stritch
Goldilocks (1958)

Sail Away
(1961)

PLATE 11

Lena Horne
Jamaica (1957)

The Lady and Her Music
(1981)

PLATE 12

Diahann Carroll
House of Flowers
(1954)

No Strings
(1962)

PLATE 13

Carol Burnett
Once Upon a Mattress
(1959)

Fade Out—Fade In
(1964)

Patti LuPone
The Robber Bridegroom
(1975)

Evita
(1978)

PLATE 15

Bernadette Peters
Sunday in the Park with George
(1984)

Into the Woods
(1987)

PLATE 16